Marshall Morgan and Scott
Marshall Pickering
3 Beggarwood Lane, Basingstoke, Hants RG23 7LP, UK

Text and illustrations © Nick Butterworth and Mick Inkpen 1988

First published in 1988 by Marshall Morgan and Scott Publications Ltd
Part of the Marshall Pickering Holdings Group
A subsidiary of the Zondervan Corporation
First published in the US by
Zondervan Publishing House, 1415 Lake Drive SE, Grand Rapids, Michigan 49506

British Library CIP Data

Butterworth, Nick
Animal tales: fox's story.
I. Title II. Inkpen, Mick
823'.914[J] PZ7

ISBN # 0-310-55790-9
Cat # 19088

Printed in Italy by Arnoldo Mondadori Editore

THE FOX'S STORY

JESUS IS BORN

Nick Butterworth and Mick Inkpen

598

ZONDERVAN

Hello, I'm a fox. I live out on the hills. I sleep by day and hunt by night.

If you're lucky you might see me on a hilltop against the moon. But don't blink or I'll be gone.

Here's my story. It'll make your tail bristle. Listen.

Two nights ago I'm up on the hill
near the town. The night is cold and
clear. I lift my head and sniff the air.
The scent of sheep is everywhere.

There's another smell too. It halts me
in my tracks. The shepherd's out...
by my nose more than one. That means
the sheep are lambing.

I skirt around the hill, then wait a while, and listen. Somewhere up ahead a lamb is calling to its mother.

Crouching low and keeping to the bushes I follow. Now I can see it clearly sitting in the long grass. A speckled lamb, not one week old.

Suddenly a blinding flash sends me running to the bushes. Shaking to my toes and blinking in the light, I freeze.

Across the hill a golden glow has fallen. And coming from the sky the sound of singing.

All at once the air is filled with shining men!

I'm scared. I cannot smell these men. They have no scent.

One of them is speaking to the shepherds.

'Don't be afraid,' he says. 'We bring good news. Great joy has come to all of you. Today in Bethlehem a baby has been born. He is your promised King, your Saviour. You'll find him lying in a manger. Quickly, run and see!'

Suddenly, the shining men are gone.
The sound of singing dies away.

The shepherds stare at one another.
Then all at once they start to talk.

They laugh and shout. They jump
and clap their hands. Then off they run
towards the town to find the baby King.
I follow on behind.

I am wary of the town. It's full of sounds and smells I do not know. But I would like to see this baby King.

Keeping to the shadows I watch the shepherds disappear inside a stable.

Behind the stable is a high fence.
Without a sound I'm up and over it.

I'm in luck. There is light
streaming through a crack in the back
wall. From here I can see everything.

Inside are cows and sheep and goats. It's odd. They know I'm here but they are not afraid.

There are people too. A woman and a man, and by the door the shepherds. All of them are looking at a manger lit by a lantern.

And there, just as the shining men said, a new-born baby sleeps. A King in a cattle shed.

His mother smiles and tells the shepherds to come in. Quietly they stand and watch. The baby murmurs in his sleep.

'His name is Jesus,' says the woman softly.

One of the shepherds takes something from his cloak. It is the speckled lamb. A present for the baby.

He gives it to the woman, then bends close to see the baby's face.

The shepherd's smiling face glows in the light, just like the shining men. He has seen a King and so have I. Not many shepherds or foxes can say that.

The shepherds whisper their goodbyes and leave.

My belly tells me that I too must be making tracks. It is a harsh winter and life is hard for a fox. And for you too, little King, it seems.

I wish you well. I hope the lamb will keep you warm. Sweet dreams.